Discovering Science

POLLUTION AND CONSERVATION

Rebecca Hunter

RAINTREE
STECK-VAUGHN
PUBLISHERS

A Harcourt Company

Austin New York
www.steck-vaughn.com

Published by Raintree Steck-Vaughn Publishers, an imprint of Steck-Vaughn Company

Acknowledgments
Project Editors: Rebecca Hunter, Pam Wells
Illustrated by Pamela Goodchild, Stefan Chabluk, and Keith Williams
Designed by Ian Winton

Planned and produced by Discovery Books

Library of Congress Cataloging-in-Publication Data
Hunter, Rebecca (Rebecca K. de C.)
Pollution and Conservation / Rebecca Hunter.
p. cm. — (Discovering science)
Includes bibliographical references and index.
ISBN 0-7398-3246-8
1. Pollution—Juvenile literature. 2. Conservation of natural resources—
Juvenile literature. [1. Pollution. 2. Conservation of natural resources.] I. Title.

TD176 .H86 2001
363.73—dc21
00-042448

2 3 4 5 6 7 8 9 0 BNG 05 04
Printed and bound in the United States of America.

Note to the reader: You will find difficult words in the glossary on page 30.

CONTENTS

OUR ENVIRONMENT

Earth is our home. It is the only planet known to support life. It provides all the food, water, and air that living things need to survive. It also provides the energy and other natural resources that humans use. All of these parts of a living thing's surroundings make up the environment.

There are three main parts of the environment, the land, the water, and the atmosphere. Plants, animals, and humans live in and use all these parts of the environment.

The Rocky Mountains show the beauty of our environment.

Each living thing is adapted, or suited, to life in its environment. If its environment changes, the living thing must also change, or it will die. Many changes that take place in an environment are caused by nature. An erupting volcano can quickly burn away all the plants in an area, destroying the environment for many years.

Pollution from factories has killed these trees.

Animals can also change an environment. A beaver will dam a stream to make a pond. The pond creates homes for some animals while destroying the riverbanks where other animals and plants live.

Many changes in the environment are caused by humans. Some of these changes are for the better, but many cause great damage.

Old fishing nets are a danger to animals like this seal.

GIVE AND TAKE

We take many things from our planet. Trees are cut down to clear the land and to make buildings, furniture, and paper. Fuels like coal, oil, and natural gas come from under the ground.

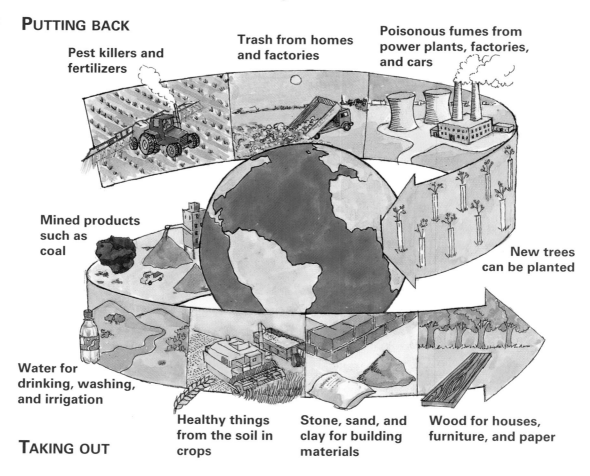

PUTTING BACK

Pest killers and fertilizers

Trash from homes and factories

Poisonous fumes from power plants, factories, and cars

Mined products such as coal

New trees can be planted

Water for drinking, washing, and irrigation

Healthy things from the soil in crops

Stone, sand, and clay for building materials

Wood for houses, furniture, and paper

TAKING OUT

We put things back into the planet, too. Sadly the things we put back are often harmful things. Factories create many poisonous waste products that go into the air, rivers, and oceans. Farmers and gardeners use insect-killing chemicals and fertilizers that rain carries into rivers. We create huge amounts of trash every day, so we must find a safe way to get rid of it.

POLLUTION AND CONSERVATION

Anything we put back into the environment that harms it or makes it dirty is called pollution. We are polluting Earth more and more every year.

Today there are more than 6 billion people in the world. This number is going to get bigger. The more people there are, the more damage is done to the world. We need to find ways to look after our planet and all our natural resources more carefully. This is called conservation.

DAMAGING THE LAND

The number of people in the world grows every day. So the people on Earth need more and more food to feed them. Farmers all over the world are looking for ways to produce more food. Many of these new ways harm the environment.

LOSS OF FORESTS

All over the world, forests have been chopped down to make room for farms. North America once had some of the largest forests in the world. Now nearly all of these have been cut down and replaced by fields and towns.

A tropical rain forest in Brazil after it was burned.

Today the areas where most trees are being destroyed are the tropical rain forests. These forests grow in places where the climate is hot and wet all year. Rain forest trees, such as teak and mahogany, provide very beautiful wood. People want this wood to make furniture.

> **WAIT A MINUTE!**
> About 150 acres (61 hectares) of rain forest are cut down every minute. At this rate, there will be no rain forests left in 100 years.

Rain forests have more types of animal and plant species than any other environment on Earth. A species is the name we give to one particular type of animal or plant. As trees are cleared, many animals and birds lose their homes. When all the members of a species die, the species becomes extinct. At least 100 species of rain forest plants and animals are becoming extinct every day.

The golden toad from Costa Rica is now extinct in the wild.

RAIN FOREST MEDICINES

Many medicines have been made from the plants in rain forests. Doctors use these to treat serious diseases, such as malaria and cancer. Scientists are discovering medicines made from plants all the time. It would be a great shame if some special plants became extinct before we discovered how they might help us.

The rosy periwinkle is a rain forest plant that is used in cancer research.

SOIL EROSION

Leaves and roots of plants protect the soil. They stop soil erosion. Erosion is when wind or rain blows or washes away soil. This soil ends up in rivers and lakes and is carried to the ocean. When too many animals feed on one area of land, the ground becomes bare and this leads to soil erosion. This is called overgrazing. Most plants cannot grow without soil. When the soil is lost, we cannot easily replace it.

◄ *This picture shows how soil has washed away after overgrazing in Mexico.*

Other harmful ways of farming can also cause erosion. In the United States in the 1930s, large dust storms blew away huge clouds of soil.

A dust storm in Colorado in 1935.

PROJECT

See how plant roots prevent erosion.

You will need

Two seed trays
Some soil
Grass seed
A watering can

1. Fill both trays with soil. Plant one tray with grass seed.

2. Keep both trays damp and wait for the seeds to sprout.

3. Wait for the grass to grow to about 2 inches (5 cm) long. (This will take 2-3 weeks.)

4. Put both trays on a steep slope, and water completely with the watering can. What happens to the soil in each case?

The soil in the tray with the grass is held in place by plant roots. The soil in the other tray will be washed away by the water.

Soil erosion on hillsides can be stopped by cutting flat steps, or terraces, like these in Bali, Indonesia.

GARBAGE

This is how much garbage the average person creates in a year:

10 times your weight in other products

90 soda cans

70 food cans

The paper from 2 trees

100 pounds (45 kg) of plastics

110 bottles and jars

Have you every thought where all this garbage goes? Many things can be recycled. Paper, plastic, metal, and glass can all be collected and made into new products. But a large amount is buried in huge holes in the ground. These are called landfills.

PROJECT

Look at the amount of glass, plastic, and paper in a bag of groceries.

You will need

A typical bag of groceries, for example:

A box of cereal

A package of cookies

A microwave TV dinner

6 cans of soda

A carton of eggs

A bottle of soft drink

A box of detergent

Use these products, but keep the containers, boxes, and packaging and do the following:

1. Weigh the containers. Do they weigh more than the contents?

2. Divide the containers into glass, metal, plastic, and paper.

3. How much packaging can be recycled? How much do you have to throw away?

In the United States, landfills cover up as much land as the whole state of Rhode Island. We are running out of places to make landfills. We need to find other ways to get rid of garbage.

LOADS OF RUBBISH
New York City throws out 24,000 tons of garbage every day!

INDUSTRIAL POLLUTION

Today we have many power plants, factories, and machines that pollute the environment. We cannot do without the energy and goods that power plants and factories create, but we can try and make the processes cleaner.

Mining does a lot of damage to the environment. At a strip mine, the top layer of soil is stripped away to reach the useful rocks. These contain minerals or fuel.

This is a coal strip mine in Great Britain.

Companies leave huge piles of waste that cover large areas of land near the mines and factories. These places can be cleaned up. If the area is covered with soil, conservation groups can plant trees and other plants and make the area ready for use by humans or animals.

LIQUID WASTE

Factories often produce many liquid waste chemicals while they make their products. Sometimes this dangerous waste is piped into the sewers. Some part of sewage is used as fertilizers for crops. Dangerous chemicals in the fertilizers could make the crops harmful. People, or other animals, who eat them could become seriously ill.

Some factories pour their liquid waste directly into nearby rivers.

AIR AND WATER POLLUTION

Factories, power plants, cars, trucks, and buses send smoke and gases into the air. These pollute the atmosphere. Air pollution causes at least 150,000 deaths a year.

Air pollution in Mexico City.

Today, the amount of smoke in the atmosphere has been reduced. But the number of other polluting gases has increased. Big industrial cities often have a layer of pollution hanging over them. In Mexico City, the air pollution is so thick that drivers often have to turn their lights on in the middle of the day.

PROJECT

Measure air pollution

You will need
A jar
A funnel
Some filter paper or paper towels
A magnifying glass
A rainy day

1. Line the funnel with the filter paper and place it in the jar.

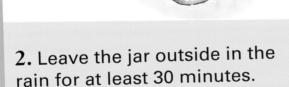

2. Leave the jar outside in the rain for at least 30 minutes.

3. Bring it in and let the filter paper dry out.

4. Examine anything that has collected on the filter paper with a magnifying glass. Can you see the dirt particles that have been washed out by the rain?

You can try this experiment in different places: a city center, a town, a park, the countryside. Which place has the dirtiest air?

OZONE

The atmosphere is the layer of gases that surrounds Earth. One of these gases is ozone. Ozone helps block out some of the Sun's harmful rays. Spray cans, fire extinguishers, air conditioning systems, and refrigerators contain chemicals that destroy the ozone layer.

There are now huge holes in the ozone layer above Antarctica and the Arctic. If these holes are allowed to get bigger, we will all be in danger from rays that can cause skin cancer.

WATER POLLUTION

Water is one of the most common substances on Earth. Life would be impossible without water. Even so, many of our water sources, including the oceans, are being slowly poisoned.

One of the biggest polluters of the ocean is sewage. Sewage should be treated before it reaches rivers or the oceans, but often it is not. If raw sewage gets into drinking water, many people become seriously ill.

Many beaches around the world are now so dirty they are unsafe for swimming.

OIL POLLUTION

Oil tankers sometimes run aground, spilling their cargo. Thousands of tons of oil can be spilled into the water in hours. The thick, black oil floats on the surface of the water. An oil spill can kill millions of ocean animals. Oil sticks to the feathers of seabirds. Then they cannot fly. If they try to clean themselves, they swallow oil that will poison them. Most oil-soaked birds die from cold or starvation.

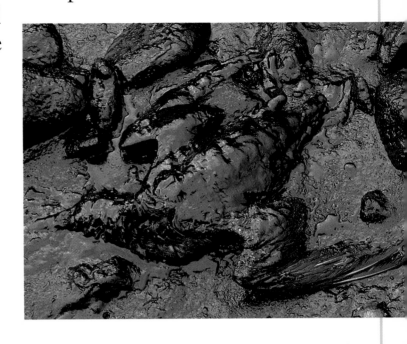

Rescue groups will try to catch and clean seabirds, but it is usually too late for most of them.

In 1989 the oil tanker Exxon Valdez *hit a reef in Alaska's Prince William Sound. It spilled 11 million gallons (42 million liters) of oil.*

WORLD PROBLEMS

GLOBAL WARMING

The world's climates are always changing. At certain times in the past, the world was much warmer than it is today. At other times, it was much colder, and ice covered huge areas of Earth. Climates change naturally, but many scientists believe that the climate today is being changed by humans.

THE GREENHOUSE EFFECT

The gases in the Earth's atmosphere work like a greenhouse. They trap the Sun's heat and warm Earth. This is called the "greenhouse effect," and it makes our planet warm enough to live on. However, today we are producing too many of the gases that trap heat that would otherwise escape into space. This may be causing the temperatures on Earth to rise.

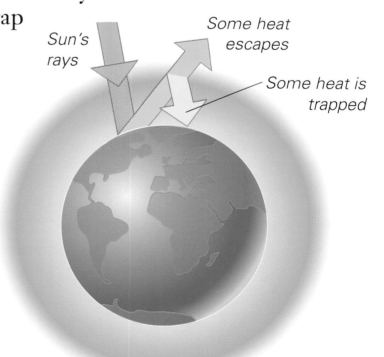

Sun's rays

Some heat escapes

Some heat is trapped

The Greenhouse Effect

You might think it would be nice to live in a warmer world. But it would not just mean better weather. As temperatures rise, ice at the North and South Poles will melt, and the sea level will rise. Many towns and cities on the coasts will be flooded.

▲ The Maldives are a group of low-lying islands. A small rise in sea level would flood them completely.

Polar animals will be the first to suffer from a loss of their habitat.

Global warming will also cause other problems. Some areas will become hotter and drier and some much wetter. These areas will suffer more from droughts and floods. It may become impossible for people to live there. As land is lost under the ocean, more people will be squeezed onto less land. We must stop polluting the atmosphere to slow down global warming.

ACID RAIN

Chemicals set free in the atmosphere by factories, power plants, and cars can pollute the rain as well as the air. This polluted rain is called acid rain.

Trees killed by acid rain.

Acid rain is poisonous to plants and can strip trees of their leaves. Whole forests can be destroyed. When acid rain reaches rivers and lakes, the plants and animals that live there begin to die. Acid rain is worst in areas with many industries, such as northern Europe and the northeastern United States.

Acid rain does not just affect the plants and animals. The stonework of buildings and statues is often damaged by it. It seeps into our water supplies and drinking water, and makes us ill.

▶ *The Church of St. Peter and St. Paul in Cracow, Poland, has been damaged by acid rain and air pollution.*

To reduce acid rain, we need to cut down on the amount of chemicals set free in the air. The burning of fuels, like coal and oil, is one of the main causes of acid rain. We should try to find cleaner energy sources that do not release chemicals into the atmosphere. We can help by using our cars less.

This helicopter is spreading a chemical called lime over a forest to combat acid rain pollution in Sweden.

WILDLIFE IN DANGER

The rate at which animals and plants are becoming extinct is now higher than ever before. Hundreds of species die out every day. Extinctions have always happened. Often they are caused by a change in climate. This is probably why the dinosaurs died out 65 million years ago.

HABITAT DESTRUCTION

Today the main cause of extinction is humans. Thousands of animals and plants are in danger because the places where they live are being destroyed. Forests are cut down and wetlands are drained to farm or build on the land. The environment is changed so much that animals and plants cannot survive.

The destruction of the Chinese bamboo forests means there are only 300-400 wild giant pandas left.

HUNTING

Hunting is another danger to wildlife. People hunt animals for food and for their fur, hide, and horns. Sometimes they hunt just for fun.

African elephants are killed for their tusks. They are a protected species, but are still being killed by poachers.

Sometimes other animals are put in danger by careless fishing methods. The fishing nets that are used to catch tuna often catch dolphins, too. Many people stopped buying cans of tuna until the fishing companies agreed to change their methods.

PLANTS IN DANGER
Many plants are also at risk from humans. Colorful flowers are used to make dyes for materials. Many orchids are in danger because people dig them up from the wild.

The largest flower in the world is almost extinct in the wild of Sumatra, Indonesia.

CONSERVATION

People all over the world are trying to halt pollution and the destruction of forests. Conservation and wildlife groups are calling on governments, businesses, and individual people to help with global conservation. Here are some of the actions that governments are taking.

The government of British Columbia, in Canada, has set aside over 10 million acres (4 million hectares) of land for the protection of animals. These animals are the caribou, grizzly bears, wolves, and buffalo.

Denmark will build 500 offshore wind power plants in a cleaner energy program. These will help reduce pollution caused by power plants burning coal or oil.

New conservation laws will protect the Galapagos Islands in the Pacific from damage by tourism and development. These laws will help safeguard giant tortoises, marine iguanas, and other species found only in the Galapagos.

Nepal has declared Kanchenjunga, the world's third highest mountain, as a special conservation area. This region is home to red pandas, snow leopards, and more than 25,000 species of flowering plants.

These and other conservation projects are helping to solve some of the environmental problems that our planet faces.

WHAT CAN YOU DO?

There are many ways in which we could make our planet cleaner and safer to live on. Each one of us can do a lot to clean up our own environment. Don't leave trash lying around. Trash is very dangerous to wildlife.

◄ *This duck is caught in the plastic rings that hold cans together.*

RECYCLING

Most towns and cities now have recycling centers. Glass, cans, paper, and some plastics can all be recycled again and again. Buying goods that are made out of recycled materials is a good idea. It will encourage more industries to make them.

SAVING ENERGY

Persuade your family to use the car less. Walk or ride your bike when you can. Save energy in the house by turning off lights or machines when they are not being used.

PROJECT

Make recycled paper

You will need

Some waste paper: newspaper, tissue, and drawing paper are all good to use
A food blender
Water
A large bowl
Some food coloring
A small picture frame
An old sheer curtain
Some thumbtacks
An adult to help

1. Tear up your wastepaper and leave it to soak in water overnight.

2. Ask the adult to help you make paper pulp by creating a liquid mash from the soaked wastepaper.

3. Fill a large bowl with paper pulp and add a few drops of food coloring if you want to make your paper colored.

Stir up the pulp. It should be as thick as cream. Add more water if necessary.

4. Tack the net over the picture frame tightly, using the thumbtacks.

5. Dip the frame in the water until it is under the surface. Turn the frame flat in the bowl and pull it out slowly. The water will drain away leaving a covering of pulp on the net.

6. Leave the frame outside to dry.

7. When the paper is totally dry, you will be able to peel it off the frame.

GLOSSARY

acid rain Rain that has become acidic because of pollution in the air. When fuels, such as oil and coal are burnt, they release gases like sulfur and nitrogen into the air. These combine with water, and fall as acid rain.

climate The usual weather in one place over a long period of time.

drought A long period with no rain.

environment The area that an animal or plant lives in. It includes everything around a living thing, such as air, soil, and water.

erosion The wearing away of Earth's surface by water, wind, or ice.

extinction The death of all the members of a species. The end of that species on our planet.

fertilizers Chemicals that are put on the land to make crops grow well.

mining The process of getting minerals or fuels out of the ground.

pesticides Chemicals that are sprayed on plants to kill pests such as insects.

terracing A way of planting to stop soil erosion. Crops are planted and grown on flat areas or steps on hillsides.

FURTHER READING

Amos, Janine. *Pollution.* (What about…? series). Raintree Steck-Vaughn, 1992.

Donnelly, Andrew. *Water Pollution.* Child's World, 1998.

Gates, Richard. *Conservation.* (New True Books). Children's, 1982.

Harlow, Rosie, and Morgan, Sally. *Pollution and Waste.* (Young Discoverers series). Kingfisher Paperbacks, 1995.

Ingpen, Robert, and Dunkle, Margaret. *Conservation: A Thoughtful Way of Explaining Conservation to Children.* Seven Hills Books, 1994.

National Wildlife Federation Staff. *Pollution: Problems and Solutions.* (Ranger Rick's Naturescope Series: Vol. 1). Chelsea House, 1999.

Patten, John M. Jr. *Polluted Air.* (Read All About Eye on the Environment series). Rourke Book Company, 1995.

The publishers would like to thank the following for permission to reproduce their pictures:

Bruce Coleman: page 4 (John Shaw), 9, top (M.P.L Fogden), 11, 21, top, 24 (Hans Reinhard), 27, top (Stafan Widstrands), bottom (Christer Fredriksson); **Corbis**: page 10, bottom; **Discovery Picture Library**: page 28, bottom; **Gettyone Stone**: Cover (Peter Cade), page 5, top and 7 (David Woodfall), 8 (Paul Edmondson), 10, top (Robert Frerck), 12 (Nick Vedros), 14 (Hans Peter Merten), 15 (Jeremy Walker), 21, bottom (Johnny Johnson), 26 (Tony Dawson); **Oxford Scientific Films**: page 5, bottom (Mark Hamblin), 9, bottom (Scott Camazine), 18 (Richard Herrmann), 19, top (Ian West), 23, bottom (Kjell-Arne Larsson), 25, top (Martyn Colbeck), bottom (Kjell Sandved), 28, top (Chris Catton); **Science Photo Library**: page 16 (Conor Caffrey), 19, bottom (Vanessa Vick), 22 and 23, top (Simon Fraser).

INDEX